MW01204316

GIFTS FROM A HEALING HEART

by Donna E. Peltz

illustrated by Terri Pennza

Harmony Press - Mentor, Ohio

Donna E. Peltz

GIFTS FROM A HEALING HEART

First Edition

Copyright 1998 by Harmony Press
All rights reserved.

Printed in the United States of America.

Library of Congress Catalog Card Number: 98-93651

ISBN   0-9667266-0-X

Cover and illustrations by Terri Pennza

Harmony Press
8596 Rosewood Lane, Mentor, Ohio 44060
Phone: 440-~~974-5479~~ 975-6112
or
~~800-794-7440~~
e-mail: donna@~~clovertel.com~~ clovertelephone.com

TABLE OF CONTENTS

ACKNOWLEDGMENTS 10
A NOTE TO THE READER 11

Chapter 1   INNER WORKINGS

BASIC BREAD   13
WINDOW POEM - anticipation   13
FINAL DAYS OF FEBRUARY   14
MARCH   15
INNER LANDSCAPE   16
OPEN DOOR   17
DIS-EASE   18
HEALING SUN   18
RED AND BLUE   19
MOURNING   20
SEA SONG   21
INNER DEPTHS   22
COFFEE OR TEA?   23
BIRTHDAY PROMISE   24
LAMB'S QUESTION   25
INDIFFERENCE   26
QUESTION   27
VIEWPOINT   27
PROPER PERSPECTIVE   28
WAR FAIR   29
SOMEDAY IS NOT A DAY OF THE WEEK   30

Chapter 2   OUTER APPEARANCES

COOKIE COMFORT   33
A MINOR MATTER   34
UNFORGOTTEN DREAM   35
TREASURELESS CHEST   36
IT FIGURES   36
DEFIANCE   36
STUBBORN STREAKS   37
PHILOSOPHY AT FORTY   38

Chapter 3   WRITE ON!

OH, YOU'RE A POET!   41
POETIC JUSTICE   42
POETIC LICENSE   43
ON GETTING RESTARTED WITH WRITING 44
WOMAN IN WINTER   45

Chapter 4   FAMILY AND FRIENDS

EVERYWOMAN   46
CRUMMY   48
MIGRATORY GRANDMA   49
PRESENCE   49
REVENGE   50
LEGACY   51
AFTER THE STROKE   52

BUTTERFLY FEELINGS 53
ED'S TRACTOR SONG 55
FEMININE AND FIFTY 56
MEMO 57
CONVERSATION WITH MOM 58
TEA TIME 61
TOGETHER. . . .FOREVER? 62
WORKING WITH THIS WOMAN 63

Chapter 5   MEN & WOMEN, WOMEN & MEN

FLOWERBED 65
DANGEROUS AGE 66
PROSPECTUS 67
ROLL PLAYING 68
GAMES 69
TRAVELOGUE 70
EYEING THE HOLE 71
ETHEREAL 72
LOVE'S CHANGING, RE-ARRANGING 73
LOVE AND A QUESTION 74
FREEDOM BOUND 75
HEALED 76
FASHIONABLE 77
ON LOVE AND MONEY 78
WEATHER 79
THE GARDEN, UPDATED 81
THEN AND NOW 82

REMEMBRANCE   83
COMING TO TERMS   84
RETIRE-EASE – PLEASE!   86
SUPPORT YOU CAN COUNT ON   87
FOR THE LOVE OF GARDENING   89

Chapter 6   SPIRITUAL JOURNEY

FOLLOWING   91
EXCHANGE   92
MY RELIGION?   93
CITATION   94
DANCING   95
CENTERING POEM: SKY   96
I AM, NOW   97
EASTER PRAYER   98
RESTORATION   100
TAKE HEART   101
WALK AWAY   102

Chapter 7   WITH GRATITUDE

GARDENING   105
LOVE   106
SONG OF LIFE   107
LOOKING AHEAD   108

ABOUT THE AUTHOR   109

ACKNOWLEDGMENTS

I wish to express my heart-felt appreciation to numerous writing friends who have consistently critiqued and continually encouraged me to persist in my work. They include: Marcella Anderson and the Monday Night Writers Group, Diane Ostrander, June Lund Shiplett, Elizabeth Vollstadt, and Barbara Whittington.

For their technical skills, insight and patience, I thank Susie Nelson, Lea Oldham, and Terri Pennza.

For the compassion, understanding, and love they gave, in allowing me to make some personal experiences public, I offer my deepest appreciation to both my mother, Coraline, and to my husband, Ed. Ed, for your special part in helping me to achieve my dream, I thank you "from the bottom of my heart."

A NOTE TO THE READER

Sometimes, in this process of living, which is truly learning how to love, we get hurt. To choose love is to be vulnerable to hurt. Daily, we listen, we laugh, we try, we cry, and we try again, until we get a little better at it. We hurt, but we heal.

It is my belief that personal hurts to the heart are necessary for growth of the spirit. When I am hurting, I transform my feelings into poems. The creative process becomes part of the healing process and, when my poem is complete, I can move ahead. Thus, the emotional hurts become gifts which help me grow in love.

Gifts are meant to be shared, so I pass them on to you, the reader. May they bring a bit more harmony, humor, joy, and love to your life.

Donna E. Peltz

Chapter One
INNER WORKINGS

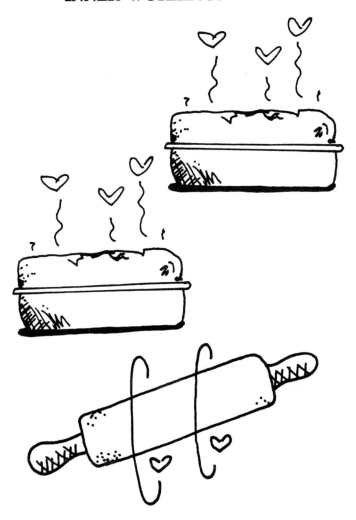

BASIC BREAD

In years gone by, a woman was held
in high esteem for her homemade bread.
Today, instead of the bread she's baking,
we treasure her for the dough she's making!

WINDOW POEM
(anticipation)

I need a wider window to the world.
I can no longer be content
with narrow confines, beauty spent.

I need a wider window to explore
how I can be more.
My soul's getting ready to fly -
Throw open the window.
I'm off to the sky!

FINAL DAYS OF FEBRUARY

Wanting to withdraw from winter,
I spin a cocoon around myself.

Snug indoors all weekend,
I concoct cotton candy clouds,
drift in dreams of daffodils,
and banter with warm breezes.

Monday morning -
I pull on my parka
and trudge through a blinding blizzard
to scrape quarter-inch ice off my windshield.

At work, I paste on a smile,
patiently answer the phone,
collate the copies,
keep up the coffee,
encourage my co-workers,
finish the filing,
and leave late, again.

In Florida, the sun is shining,
but neither God nor FEDEX delivers it here!

"Triple A?"
"Could I get a ticket to Tampa tomorrow?"

MARCH

In green-remembered pastures, blackbirds sing.
My soul would, too, were it not wintered in.

But talk of drugs, disease and acid rain
immobilize me in my chair again.

Caring should arouse me from despair,
and crocuses should shake me with a start,

yet outdoors, blackened snow still clumps the ground
while indoors, curtained windows web my heart.

Until I sight a redwing flitting by,
my inner landscape's locked in winter's eye.

INNER LANDSCAPE
A tribute to Andrew Wyeth

Why do I keep seeing Wyeth land
more clearly than the land beyond my sill?

In universal views of rural life,
he opens up our eyes to see his world.

With poignancy and courage, his works show
appearances deceive, as we all know.

To grasp life's barren beauty, look again:
Life is love, reflected from within.

OPEN DOOR

Always leave a door ajar
for someone to come in.
A person who has left your life
may want back in again.

The one who closed his mind to you,
who turned and walked away,
may one day change his point of view
and hear what you would say.

One never knows, for Fate is strange,
how circumstance or mind will change.
So always leave an open door,
for love needs room to come once more.

DIS-EASE

A friend of mine is doctoring for ulcers.
Another one just had a D & C.

We drive ourselves
with stress
to death.

If we nourished our bodies on inner peace,
would we still eat our hearts out, piecemeal?

HEALING SUN

As butterflies are drawn to flowers,
so we are drawn by mystic powers -
to earth and plants, fresh air and sky;
we heal ourselves in sun-drenched hours.

RED AND BLUE

I am my mother.
You are, too.
Easily hurt,
we break in two.

So, tell me, Love,
what shall we do -
we overly sensitive,
easily blue?

Maybe we'd better
be spunky red.
Why care
what's in another's head?

We need to keep
our own hearts strong.
Trusting our hearts,
we won't go wrong.

Impervious we,
to their taunting song -
spunky and red
our whole lives long!

MOURNING

I watch a paper whipping on the road
become a mourning dove as I approach.
Too late to stop, I cringe and drive ahead.

I try to blot its image from my mind.
I can't.
Still, it squawks before my inner eye.

Displaced and desperate in a world of wheels,
it struggles for the shelter of the sky.
I struggle to forget. . . .

I drove by.

SEA SONG

I healed myself with sea and sand
along the ocean's shore -
refound myself, explored myself,
restored myself once more.

I have my friends, I have myself,
I have the warmth of sun
and, now attuned to ebb and flow,
my music's just begun!

INNER DEPTHS

I shall arise when the sun is low.
I shall arise to the silent snow.
I shall arise, leaving warmth of bed
and journey to meet myself, instead.

Who am I truly? And what can I do?
Fears are familiar; exploring is new.

But I'm getting older and I must know
which dreams to keep and which let go. . . .

Angels, be with me through winter cold.
Shine light on my path as I grow old!

COFFEE OR TEA?

When today has ended,
will we have steamed, sputtered,
and finally boiled over
like coffee percolating in a pot -
Or will we have been calming
and comforting as chamomile tea,
soothing one another's souls
and looking back in love?

BIRTHDAY PROMISE

Many years I've been a mother;
many more I've been a wife -
chose to be responsive, giving,
putting others first in life. . . .

Fifty-seven birthday candles
promise so much more to be:
Time to take my dreams off "hold" now -
Time has come for loving me!

LAMB'S QUESTION

April, begrudgingly, lets go of snow,
but speaks her mind through gales that blow.
Hills wear winter gray today.

But, lamb that I am, I keep seeing in my head
Earth aglow in sunshine
wearing spring grass green, instead.

In pastures, I am leaping.
How long must Spring lie sleeping?

INDIFFERENCE

Everyone has horrid days,
I judge from what I've read.

The world, though brown, still turns around
as I emerge from bed.

It does not care if my soul despairs
and wastes its winter hours.

Indifferently, it goes its way
preparing for spring flowers.

QUESTION

I'm a woman through and through
under pressures, sane as you.
I wonder, if I crack in two,
will God repair with Super Glue?

VIEWPOINT

Life's not fully black
nor entirely white.
No one's fully bad.
No one's fully right.

Life tends to be varied -
sometimes it is gray.
Sometimes it's rose-tinted,
a pink, pastel day.

Or maybe, life only
appears that way,
for God made this world
and He loves to play!

PROPER PERSPECTIVE

There is a pattern in our lives
I do not understand.
Some people let their needs for wealth
soon gain an upper hand.
They're rarely ever satisfied
with treasures laid in store.
From dawn to dusk, they drive themselves
forever seeking more.

It seems to me it isn't gold
that matters in the end,
but love and understanding
and someone to be my friend.

I'm glad I have some money,
but I thank the Lord above
that I've been blessed with more than gold,
that I've been blessed with love.

WAR FAIR

Firing a plastic gun,
my young son
plays guerrilla warfare.

Costumed in khaki,
a canteen on his belt,
he and his dog track down the enemy.

Elsewhere in the world,
our television shows us,
people are not playing.

Too soon, I know, Uncle Sam,
who won't be playing, either,
will knock on our door.

I wish. . . .
but wishes don't work.

In a war fair world,
my son becomes his gun

as the Earth which gave him breath
now lures him back in games of death!

SOMEDAY IS NOT A DAY OF THE WEEK

How many promises broken?
How many dreams tucked away?
How many goals put on hold now,
to wait for a less busy day?

How many friendships have faded?
How many loves ran awry?
How many words went unspoken
because there'd be time, by 'n by?

Dreams are for sharing together.
Castles need building today.
Too soon the sunrise is setting.
Let's live in the present, today!

Chapter Two
OUTER APPEARANCES

COOKIE COMFORT

I have a love affair with food.
I eat when I am in the mood.

Forget about a calorie zone -
I much prefer a cheese calzone.

And pizza, too, will sometimes do,
or dark rich chocolates - take two!

It isn't that I haven't tried
to put my fattening tastes aside,
but the rabbit in me died!

I'd eat my veggies and I'd run;
I'd count my fat grams - not much fun -

but still I found that in the end
a comfort food was my best friend.

Today, I love my chubby self,
and cookies rate a special shelf

within my cupboard, by the tea.
I am content as I can be -
with cookies, life tastes good to me!

A MINOR MATTER

What's important is they are healthy -
my two "fried eggs,"
so-called by my lover, who wishes
        they were "grapefruits!"

If I had a mastectomy, no one would know -
unless I pointed it out verbally,
since I don't point out physically.

We women who strive for equal rights
        must acknowledge
that all women were not created equal,
a minor matter in the eyes of God. . . .

Ah, that this were so in the eyes of men!

UNFORGOTTEN DREAM

For thirty-nine years, I've had this dream
of being thin.
Not skinny as a Vogue model, but streamlined -
specifically, ten pounds thinner
than I always seem to be.

I've been there before, briefly. . . .
radiant at what I'd accomplished
proud of my slim silhouette
    looking trim and neat in my junior petite,
    by-passing sundaes for black coffee.

Yet always, coaxing me to the kitchen,
are cookies.
So always, leering at me from the closet,
are my larger sizes.

For thirty-nine years, I've had this dream. . . .
Will I make it by forty?
Or, will I make forty
and change my dream?

TREASURELESS CHEST

I jog and there's little to jiggle.
I'm braless - there's little to bounce.
Perfume they never were meant to contain,
so why do we treasure each ounce?

IT FIGURES

Designer jeans no longer seem
what Bill Blass had in mind
for the woman over thirty
with a redesigned behind!

DEFIANCE

Gray hairs come most unexpected;
They would put me in my place.
I'll defy them; I will dye them -
Better dye than age with grace!

STUBBORN STREAKS

Despise your gray?
Wash it away.
Disguise it, blend it,
simple, they say.

I wash and find
when I am done
I still detect
each stubborn one.

It's not just their color
that makes me frown,
but the fact that the gray ones
refuse to lie down!

PHILOSOPHY AT FORTY

When I was ten plus thirty,
I heard a poet say,
Give sage advice and recipes,
but not your age away.

Give quips and quotes and accolades
and promises galore,
but never give your age away,
if you would know the score!

Admitting that you're forty, Dear,
is comparable to treason
for once you reach that mellow age,
it's always open season!

Your hands will need that Ivory touch,
your skin will need Camay;
your face, to keep its youthful look,
needs Oil of Olay.

As for your hair, you need not swear
if you dislike the gray -
you simply use some Loving Care
to wash it all away.

At forty, I'm concerned with fat,
but chocolate is where it's at!
A wedge of Brie, a glass of wine,
good friends to share, I'm feeling fine!

Let Youth wear Avon purple eyes
and Levi jeans of 4/5 size;
at forty, I choose Comfort-stride
and wear size 12/14 with pride.

At forty, I would simplify -
I like my wine and humor dry.
An optimist, I believe the sage
who promises life improves with age!

Chapter Three
WRITE ON!

OH, YOU'RE A POET!

A poet?
Who knows?
Who dares suppose?

Before you call
yourself a poet,
show it.

Write, rewrite your best
then put them to the test
of time.

Whose words endure?
Do yours?
Do mine?

I versify and write such prose
my words may sometimes curl your toes,
but as for calling myself a poet. . . .
Let centuries pass, and then I'll know it!

POETIC JUSTICE

The price is high
to be a poet.
(Is this why we are so few?)
All writers know it.

Poets are paid
not in dollar nor penny
but in sample copies
of which we get many.

We're poor. We're vain:
we pay a mint
to simply see
our names in print!

POETIC LICENSE

Much of me resists the rules:
be logical, concise.
What writers' self-created god
makes poets pay the price?

Now, I'm a rebel writer.
I often use free verse.

I toss in rhyme
from time to time

(Circle one:)

A) which usually makes things worse.
B) to blend them both in a new design.
C) I've written a better ending
    which I'm mailing to the poet.

If you circled "C" above, please check one:

__I'm enclosing a SASE which enables me
to receive my own poetic license, absolutely free.

__I don't wish to receive a poetic license at this time,
    but please read my ending anyhow.

ON GETTING RESTARTED WITH WRITING
(perusing and procrastinating with my muse)

My muse is at me again
distracting me from chores at hand
attracting me to my typewriter stand
hounding me once again to begin
the bothersome, daily discipline

confounding me with creative choices
seducing me with her siren voices
provoking me - yes, I know I should write
revoking me, "In the name of God: now!"

Holy Cow, can you tell me how?
When I'm needing a nap?
I'm short on sleep
and writing will keep. . . .

Poems on ice
are nice!

WOMAN IN WINTER

Perhaps my work will keep.
Will I?

Knuckles gnarl.
Arches ache.
Forty feels fifty.

Writing waits
as winter whistles by.
Will I die a pregnant poet
or deliver, overdue?

Time will tell
if dreams can keep.
Tonight, I tire;
tonight, I'll sleep
and dream of poems, done.

Chapter Four
FAMILY AND FRIENDS

EVERYWOMAN

My cousin Jo, who ought to know,
says her friends are only two.
That's too few. She knows this, too,
but doesn't know what she can do
to change or rearrange her life -
She's family-driven, mother, wife.

Outside her home, she's office help
some forty hours a week.
Add grocery shopping, laundry, meals,
she's running eighty, peak.

We spoke of this the other day,
during time we'd snatched for play.
Then I grabbed car keys - had to run.
I said, "Joann, this has been fun!
Let's plan to meet next Saturday
to see if we can find a way
to put more pleasure in our lives. . . .
perhaps be less than perfect wives.

"We nurture by nature.
We give 'til we're poor,
and though others need us,
we need ourselves more."

Our simple conclusion? Let's make time for tea,
for I am Joann and Joann's truly me.
We're each Everywoman who ever will be,
and teatime is our time to live joyfully.

CRUMMY

Lord, how I loathe
baking cookies!

Clubs need them.
Kids need them.

I don't need them!

I used to mix them and bake them
and snitch them and gain

until I met a newly-wed
who clearly and succinctly said,

"I don't bake!"

What a notion!
Trying her potion,

I no longer mix them.
I no longer bake them.

I no longer snitch them and gain!

Lord, how I love
NOT baking cookies!

MIGRATORY GRANDMA

Grandma was always arriving
or departing,
suitcase in hand.

Fussing over fly-away hair,
she'd preen before the hallway mirror -
as if arranging accessories
would somehow arrange her life!

PRESENCE

My mother's gone away,
but she's more with me today
than she is when she's physically near -
three thousand miles from home,
    she's still too here!

REVENGE

I envy robins flying South,
for I am a mother who would abandon her nest
to sight a Southern sunrise,
alone.

No, robins do not desert;
they fly in a family flock.

And I, like them, am bound to my brood,
eternally maternal being that I am.

But beware -
I'm coming back as a cat!

LEGACY
(to my young daughter)

I'd like to run away from you -
set out alone and disappear,
but your brown eyes would follow me,
entreating, haunting, like a deer.

Persistently, you rub me wrong,
and constantly, we disagree.
I'm led into your verbal traps,
when, in my mind, I would walk free.

The reservoir of love I knew
evaporates from day to day
as you distract and prickle me;
you mire me in child's play.

With learned finesse, you taunt my soul.
You pilfer patience it would know.
But then you smile. My heart forgives.
I'm won with velvet eyes of doe.

Why is it, as I sense some sun,
you dart to deeper woods anew?
I only hope a deer-eyed child
shall one day dapple trails for you!

AFTER THE STROKE

How do you carry on
when the Mom you knew is gone?

Though Mom still has her body
and most all of her mind,
her Spirit has been broken
and it cannot find "re-wind."

We live together peaceably.
We're loving and we're kind.
But will we ever know again
the joy we left behind?

BUTTERFLY FEELINGS

Today I choke
on words I spoke,

for I have crushed a butterfly
of fragile feelings, made her cry.

I lost my patience, was unkind -
lost my love and lost my mind.

Now there is hurt I must erase,
and I'm the one who must replace

a spirit sad, devoid of love
with healing, white light from Above.

A hug, a smile, a tender touch
are what I give. May they mean much.

May she forgive and set me free,
so we can live in harmony

and love, as God would have us be -
restored, and living gracefully.

ED'S TRACTOR SONG

I sit upon my tractor
and I sing a happy song.
I dig holes with my tractor
and I'm happy all day long.

I love my yellow tractor
'cause it makes a joyful noise.
It rumbles loudly as I work
and brings me many joys.

I dig a hole into the ground.
I dig it very deep.
I bury tree stumps, bricks and blocks
I do not wish to keep.

I also dig a drainage ditch
where water soon will flow,
so I can have a dry back yard -
and lots more grass to mow.

I work hard with my tractor
and I sing a happy song.
I dream dreams with my tractor,
and I'm glad that summer's long!

FEMININE AND FIFTY

We are sisters, you and I,
swept beneath a storm-tossed sky

alike in very many ways,
seeking passion in our days.

Pent-up feelings stuffed within
will keep no more. We thirst again.

We're filled with mystery and love
and changing as the sky above.

We've wider worlds we must explore.
We're Phoenix, and we rise once more!

MEMO

"Remember, you are loved," the magnet read.
I mailed it to Mom.
My mother is old and sometimes she forgets.

"Remember, you are loved," my letter said.
I mailed it to my daughter.
My daughter is young and sometimes she forgets.

"Remember, you are loved," we promised true.
I worry. Careless words cut love in two.
We're middle-aged. Are we forgetting, too?

CONVERSATION WITH MOM

Yesterday, Mother was bustling and bright.
Since her stroke, she contends
with an arm not right.

"You're okay," we children say.
"Just thank God you're alive today!"

"It's just something that happened -
nothing you could control.
Your brain controls your muscles.
We love you for your soul!"

"Tell me, how can you love me?
I'm not who I used to be.
I cry and cry,
and I don't know why.

"I'm okay, you say. I'm not to blame.
Well, what has happened to my brain?
And, as long as I live,
will my arm be lame?"

"So many of my friends have passed away. . . .
Living here, I'm only in your way.
Maybe one of my troubles is not enough sun,
so tomorrow, I'm packing to get me some.

"I'll leave you to your gray Ohio day.
You live as you see fit. Do things your way.
I hope you get your drive poured 'fore the snow,
but if it don't get done, I needn't know.

"And you ought to unshovel
     that dirt dumped on your tree,
but then that's up to you and not to me
I'm not trying to tell you what to do.
I only know, with what I been through,
I just can't take these winters and the cold.
You mark my words: It's no fun growing old!"

TEA TIME

It's time for tea
for you and me,
a friendly time
to simply be -
to slow the hurried pace of day.

It's tea time -
time to break away
into a space of solitude
to calm our soul and mend our mood. . . .

Muffins, friendship, you and me:
the world's made right as we sip tea!

TOGETHER. . . .FOREVER?

I can be here.
I can be there.
Why, I can be just anywhere!

I can do this.
I can do that.
Why, I can wear just any hat!

I can jump high.
I can jump low.
I can go any way but slow!

I'll shine your shoes,
shampoo your hair,
and take you with me everywhere.

But when I've lost my sanity
who will there be to care for me?
And since I won't be there for you,
will God or Medicare come through?

WORKING WITH THIS WOMAN

Me, thinking to myself,
    Two females working together?
    The Dear Lord knows we try:
    She holds her tongue;
    I bite my lip
    as one more day goes by.

Collectively, we sigh
and ask the Dear Lord,
    "Why?"

We then hear God reply
    "Ladies, life is a test.
    Therefore, do your best.
    And remember your sense of humor -
    Better a laugh than a tumor!"

Chapter Five
MEN & WOMEN, WOMEN & MEN

FLOWERBED
(Dedicated to May Sarton)

Have I gardened
too long
to flower myself?

Beside a pinstriped hybrid bloom
I nurtured seedlings
to strong starts.

Side by side
we grew
until we crowded.

I'll separate -
delve deeper,
stretch sunward.

Watered with love
from feminine friends,
my own fruition
may be possible.

DANGEROUS AGE

My friends warn,
"A man in his forties
needs watching."

My competition
turns out to be
a generous dish

of vanilla ice cream
coupled with
the lure of the late, late show.

I'm warning friends,
"A woman in her forties
needs watching!"

PROSPECTUS

Because I have a good marriage,
grown monotonous,
I gaze at you.

Because your virile body excites,
because your teasing word invites,
I imagine an affair with you:

We escape on a bike,
race to the sun,
wear wind on our backs, worry-free.

But, because, years ago, you married her,
and, because, years ago, I married him,
we are caught in commitments today

and I shall do nothing about us
but ponder
and write poems.

ROLL PLAYING

I want to be writing
instead of cooking.

Between blending and stirring,
I swallow black coffee, standing.

The man I married
sits and sips.

Once, with company coming,
he concocted Caesar salad -
gargantuan with garlic,
indelibly inedible.

Since that salad,
I squander my minutes
preparing our food -
while the poet in me starves.

Would words nourish his body,
were I to nourish my mind?

GAMES

Something's amiss -
I miss your kiss,

your hearty, "Hi!"
your wave good-bye,

your, "See you soon -
I'll call at noon!"

You'll torment
long as I will grieve.

I feign a smile
as love takes leave!

TRAVELOGUE

On our way West
he is distant,
inaccessible,
cold as jagged icy peaks
until his anger thunders through
and amassed hatreds
pound me like hail.

We head home,
and in the heavy silence,
my heart searches for softness,
but my mind finds granite rocks.

EYEING THE HOLE

Before marriage, we disagreed over donuts.
Offering friendship, I left some in your locker.
You refused them; you refused me.

How could I let this be?
We were to share a life,
to live as man and wife.

I broke the silence and spoke.
We moved ahead with hope.

Before divorce, we again disagree over donuts.
In a facade of friendship, you bring some home.
I refuse them; I refuse you.
I have learned. To myself I'm true!

You never showed me love nor care.
Today's a little late to share!

Today, words stay unspoken;
our lifeline has been broken -
but we have donuts everywhere,
a crumbling, ironical token!

ETHEREAL

Our flower of love has shriveled dry
and, feeling past the need to cry,
I gather its petals one by one
and fling them upward to the sun,
willing them regroup on high
and come back as a butterfly
that beauty of a transient thing
next time enhance the earth on wing!

LOVE'S CHANGING, RE-ARRANGING
(a self-portrait in three parts)

FIRST, THE CHANGE

A stranger now you have become,
though I knew you once, when we were young,
when hand in hand, we shared the sun
and walked in the rain and loved as one.

Then work won you over and jobs were done,
sun after sun, after sun, after sun
until money was God, was you, was one.
Uncoupled we stood, our harmony done.

NEXT, A CONCLUSION

Alone by myself
I would rather be,
for when we are us
there is still just me.

FINALLY, MOVING AHEAD

Now I walk my own byways and sing my own songs
and I've learned, in my second-hand style,
about darkness and sunlight and laughter and love.
Life is good. I am strong, and I smile.

LOVE AND A QUESTION

How suddenly beautiful moments are born:
a delicate rainbow, a dark summer storm,
a sandpiper's cry at the edge of the sea,
a moment of love for two friends such as we.

Yet, as we watch them, the sandpipers fly
and rainbows dissolve at the edge of the sky;
storm clouds blow over and summers will end. . . .
Do lovers continue forever, dear friend?

FREEDOM BOUND

Kite, sailng high in a washed blue sky,
my lover and I are as equally free.

It's deceptive to be
caught constantly,

by a single, residual thread!

HEALED

No, I will not see you again.

We shared sunlight, overcast with shadows.
We shared time, stolen from others.

You're gone and I am free now.
I'm stronger, much more me now.

Today, I choose friends
who will shine in the sun.

You're a cloud from my past -
and we're done!

FASHIONABLE

After all is said and done
I tell myself that we had fun.

But was it more than just a lark?
Did we ever know fire in the dark?

Our love, dear friend, was a glowing coal,
but never a passion to stir the soul.

Is love ever more? I wish I knew
for somehow I sense a lack with you.

This is I know, though, I love brooks
and lakes and oceans and trees and books.

I love peaches and beaches and life with a passion.
Maybe loving a man just isn't my fashion!

ON LOVE AND MONEY

If I can't find the perfect love,
I'll settle for lots of money.

But 'til the day my ship comes in,
I'll let you be my honey.

If I can't find the perfect love,
I'll love the honey I find,

but on the day my ship comes in,
you may not find it funny

to find yourself in second place,
outranked by the perfect money!

WEATHER

The rains came down relentlessly
and raged into a storm.
The thunder roared, the lightning seared -
relationships were torn.

And when the storm had spent itself,
I stood upon the shore,
a solitary soul washed clean
now well and calm once more.

I questioned if I'd ever have
again a chance to care;
in later rain, the rainbows came
and brought us time to share.

In sunny days, with gentle ways,
you helped me to grow strong,
for storm clouds end and rainbows bend
when love lifts life in song.

We all need times of weathering
to shape and stretch the soul.
Give thanks for storms, for songs, for love -
for storm-tossed, we grow whole.

THE GARDEN, UPDATED

She said:
  Placement of a flowerbed ought not to be fought.
  Nevertheless, a bed should be planned
  so it wouldn't be crammed
  in a too small space
  and appear out of place
  between the grill and the awning wall,
  a triangular bed, in a place too small.

He said:
  Aesthetically, do you not see
  we need a bit of color there?
  Or, otherwise, we only stare
  at gray concrete within that space.
  A small tree won't be out of place.
  And flowers will just add some class.
  We'll do it, Dear. Your mood will pass.

God said:
  There is always room for beauty to bloom.
  Open your closed mind to spaces -
  I do my best work in tight places.
  And love needs both gardens and graces!

THEN AND NOW

I played fifth chair clarinet.
Charles played first.
Three years younger than I,
he played ever so much better. . . .
and Charles was a guy.

Today, I spell well.
An elderly, mis-spent English teacher,
I now write glorious, grammatically correct
thank-you letters to customers.

Again, I am support to younger men,
the guys who sell
so wonderfully well
to sexy feminine secretaries
who phone us for their male bosses
who inherently wield the power
to hire and to fire
secretaries who spell well.

REMEMBRANCE

You think you know me, I can tell.
The truth is you don't know me well.

For I've had lovers, same as you,
who served their purpose, saw me through

those times in which I had to grow....
one happened several years ago:

I was younger, in my prime.
Though transitory, joy was mine.

Together, we shared wine, the beach
when permanence was out of reach.

Our joy was seasonal at best;
commitment never was a test.

So, when the sun set, we walked on
in separate paths, to greet the dawn

not dreaming on some future day
we'd all shake hands and smile and say,

"How do you do? You're looking fine!"
Yes, you with yours and I with mine,
making small talk, sipping wine.

I'm wintered now, I'm warm, content
but I remember spring, well-spent!

COMING TO TERMS

It used to be that our tv,
tuned extra loud, would bother me.

The picture screen and extra noise
would seem to steal all my joys.

But now I've come to like tv,
for tv time's my time to be

curled into a comfy nook
lost in wonder with a book.

I'm apt to travel anywhere,
for armchair pilots take me there.

I've come to terms with what's ahead;
Ed loves tv; I love my Ed.

(He even plays it while in bed;
I think it helps him clear his head.)

I don't know how this came to be -
that tv doesn't bother me.

For me, it's not priority;
I've other things to do and see,
yet we both live quite peaceably.

We each are where we want to be:
I have my books; Ed has tv.

We co-exist most happily,
for I'm with Ed and Ed's with me.

Thus ends my verse, but not tv!

RETIRE-EASE - PLEASE!

My man is now retired
which explains why I am just plain tired!
But if I am tired more than once
am I retired too?

Heavens! That would *never* do!
For with just we two
there is *work* to be done
and it's truly no fun
being the dumped-on one -
me, the light of his life. . . .
This perpetuates strife!

The solution, I think, is:
A wife needs a wife!

SUPPORT YOU CAN COUNT ON

Forever, I'm told:
Support your guy!

Why?

Can't suspenders support him
far better than I?

———————————

P.S. I purchase a pair
and put them in a box
with a card that reads:

"Your loving wife.
Now you shall have the support you need
to last you the rest of your life."

FOR THE LOVE OF GARDENING

Young ladies have lovers.
Middle-aged ladies have gardens.
And old ladies, having learned to love gardens,
have gardeners.

Since gardens need love,
old ladies should have gardeners
who love to garden,
and do it well.

And since ladies of every age, even old ladies,
need love,
they should have gardeners
who double as lovers,
and do it well.

Or do their gardeners just love gardening?

Whatever their status,
I won't tell.
Years ago Love began in a garden. . . .
and still grows well!

Chapter Six
SPIRITUAL JOURNEY

FOLLOWING

I think it is okay to write
a thought that doesn't come out right.
A concept that's unfinished yet
is one I'm working on to get
just right.
I write
and as I put words down
they choose to change
and rearrange.
I follow and to my delight
when they are done,
my writing's right.

So, too, the winding way of God
seems not to be the path I'd take,
but I have learned, from writing words,
to follow, for my own heart's sake.

God knows a grander point of view -
a place He wants to lead me to.
To follow words does not seem odd.
Can I do less than follow God?

EXCHANGE

I'm gonna hand my unhappiness,
like an old shoe,
over to God.

God, being God,
has no need to be shod,
or happy or blue,
as we humans do.

So, what'll God do,
being stuck with my shoe?

Will He toss it away,
and send sunshine my way?

Lordy, I wish I knew -
shoes wear through!

MY RELIGION?

I'm a runner.
I'd rather be running than
chanting in church.

Running is my ritual.
It is rationale.
It is right for me.

I rhyme as I run.
I fuse and become
my surroundings.

Today, I am sun.
Omniscient, I hum.

I am Light.
I am Love.
I am One.

CITATION

Siren screaming behind me,
I pull to the side of the road.

A big, burly policeman
fills my window.

"You were speeding, Lady!
"The limit through here is 25 miles an hour."

I could say:
    Hurrying has become a habit, Officer.
    I hurry to work. I hurry to meetings. I hurry home.
    I never slow down to ask myself why.
    Likely, I'll be in a hurry to die.

All excuses,
so I say nothing.

Is this ticket a wake-up call from God?

DANCING

I would choose to dance with God -
but not follow, I would lead,
so God let me dance alone
until I did one day plead,

"Not tomorrow, but today -
I'll follow, God. You lead the way."

Where would He lead? What must I do?
I long to dance, but I'm fearful to.

But God's unlimited! Am I, too?
Maybe we'll dance until I grow new,
over the rainbow and out of view!
I'm going dancing! Will you come, too?

CENTERING POEM: SKY

Focus on the sky above you.
Center on a patch of blue.
Focus on the clouds and sky-lake;
sky and lake will see you through.

Focus on the cloud above you:
sail to it; be as one.
Fly forth from your earthly body;
energize it with the sun.

Sun is light, is love, is purpose.
Sun is life, is God, is One;
harmony blends mind and spirit. . . .
Life is living to Become.

I AM, NOW

Focus on your higher selfhood.
Center on the Christ within.
Breathe in deep to drink in calmness;
let yourself be whole again.

In the past, you glimpsed a vision
where your higher self would lead.
Time is now to manifest it,
render dream from thought to deed.

In this time of seeming darkness,
you must keep your vision bright.
Set your mind to be illumined;
flood your soul with love and light.

Even now you have the power.
Be the person you would be.
Act without, the Christ within you.
Know you are and know you're free!

EASTER PRAYER

"Father, forgive them
for they know not what they do."
Father, forgive me,
for I am as those two -

I hurt the very ones I love
without intending to;
I would my heart o'erflowed with love,
but I'm imperfect, too,
and far too often, I don't see
another's point of view.

God grant me patience that I keep
your gentle ways and wise,
for I would know the hurting heart
and see through troubled eyes.

And help me, God, to live in love
when I don't understand,
and keep me ever open
to the lesson that's at hand.

I know that we are here to learn
of unconditioned love,
so keep me focused on Your Light
that I may rise above
the stubbornness of being right -
Transpose my mind with love.

Forgive me, Lord, and teach me love
as only You can do.
Transform me, change me with Your love,
for I am as those two.

RESTORATION

Above the clouds, the sun is bright.
Below the clouds is rain and gray.
God plays with rainbows, dark and light
to give us hope along our way.

When life dumps rain, I tend to be
depressed at times, untrue to me.
God bids me fly above the rain
that I may laugh and love again.

In search of joy and harmony,
I seek the sun to set me free.
Restored, I've balance, vibrancy.
I rest in God; God shines through me!

TAKE HEART

Do not be consumed by heartache.
Life is ever growth and pain;
sunlight dapples in the darkness,
joy knows passion in the rain.

Therefore, keep your vision focused
during shadows of the sun -
know and trust your inner wisdom,
knowing you and God are One.

WALK AWAY!

"Walk away," my dear friend said.
Her words still echo in my head.

Even Jesus in His day
left the multitudes to pray.

In the hubbub of the day,
He knew His needs and slipped away.

Do not care what people say.
When you need to, walk away.

True, some folks will think you rude
when you seek your solitude.

Doesn't matter what's at hand.
When you need to, take a stand.

Leave the crises and the phone.
Excuse yourself to be alone.

Go within and talk to God.
Doesn't matter you seem odd.

Deep within your quiet heart
God has wisdom to impart.

Each of us needs sacred ground.
God speaks in silence, I have found.

Deep within our solitude,
God centers us and calms our mood.

It matters not what others say.
Leave the chaos of the day.

When you feel the need to pray,
be like Jesus - Walk away!

Chapter Seven
WITH GRATITUDE

GARDENING

Yesterday, I took for granted
love would flourish in our home.

I thought, Love needs no gardener's touch -
Love's strong enough to stand alone.

But seasons teach a gardener much
and, weathered, I now know

that Love, most fragile of all blooms,
needs constant care to grow!

LOVE

Love is, daily, the gift we give.
Love is, in action, the way we live.
Love is always being there
to share both triumphs and despair.
Love gives thanks for joy and sorrow.
Love looks forward to tomorrow.
Love is listening with the heart.
Love is forgiving and restart.
Love chooses kindness, rather than right.
Love chooses humbleness, rather than might.
Love chooses faith, instead of fears.
Love teaches peace throughout the years.
Trusting in love, we dissipate doubt:
Love is for living, from inside to out.

SONG OF LIFE

Life is once both joy and sorrow -
sunlight dappled midst the rain -
loneliness, and, if we're lucky,
one more chance to love again.

So sing - that song cannot be ended
when it never has been sung. . . .
and love - a love cannot be ended
when it never has begun!

LOOKING AHEAD

For all the brilliant thoughts I've had
and all the words I've said,
I do believe the best to be
still wait within my head!

ABOUT THE AUTHOR

Donna E. Peltz has been a teacher, a mother, a sales person, a secretary, and always, a writer. Throughout the years, she has shared her poems with those closest to her.

Her work has appeared in American Legion, Kyriokos, the Unitarian Universalist Women's Federation Journal, Living with Children, Marriage and Family Living, Women's Circle Home Cooking, Light Year, 1986, by Bits Press of Case Western Reserve University and, most recently, Reflections from a Mud Puddle, by Boyds Mills Press.

In addition to writing, Donna enjoys jogging, bike riding, and traveling. She resides with her husband and her mother in Mentor, Ohio, where she is currently working on her next book.

She can be contacted by writing to: Harmony Press, 8596 Rosewood Lane, Mentor, Ohio 44060 or via e-mail at: donna@clovertel.com

See page 5